ALL AROUND THE WORLD
MOROCCO

by Kristine Spanier, MLIS

Ideas for Parents and Teachers

Pogo Books let children practice reading informational text while introducing them to nonfiction features such as headings, labels, sidebars, maps, and diagrams, as well as a table of contents, glossary, and index.

Carefully leveled text with a strong photo match offers early fluent readers the support they need to succeed.

Before Reading

- "Walk" through the book and point out the various nonfiction features. Ask the student what purpose each feature serves.
- Look at the glossary together. Read and discuss the words.

Read the Book

- Have the child read the book independently.
- Invite him or her to list questions that arise from reading.

After Reading

- Discuss the child's questions. Talk about how he or she might find answers to those questions.
- Prompt the child to think more. Ask: People in Morocco celebrate independence every year. Do you celebrate your country's independence? How?

Pogo Books are published by Jump!
5357 Penn Avenue South
Minneapolis, MN 55419
www.jumplibrary.com

Library of Congress Cataloging-in-Publication Data

Names: Spanier, Kristine, author.
Title: Morocco / by Kristine Spanier.
Description: Minneapolis: Jump!, 2021.
Series: All around the world | Includes index.
Audience: Ages 7-10 | Audience: Grades 2-3
Identifiers: LCCN 2019043096 (print)
LCCN 2019043097 (ebook)
ISBN 9781645273417 (hardcover)
ISBN 9781645273424 (paperback)
ISBN 9781645273431 (ebook)
Subjects: LCSH: Morocco–Juvenile literature.
Classification: LCC DT305 .S73 2021 (print)
LCC DT305 (ebook) | DDC 964–dc23
LC record available at https://lccn.loc.gov/2019043096
LC ebook record available at https://lccn.loc.gov/2019043097

Editor: Jenna Gleisner
Designer: Molly Ballanger

Photo Credits: Seleznev Oleg/Shutterstock, cover; federico neri/Shutterstock, 1; Pixfiction/Shutterstock, 3; simruhc/iStock, 4; stockstudioX/iStock, 5; saiko3p/Shutterstock, 6-7; Jiang Chaoyang/EyeEm/Getty, 8-9; HUANG Zheng/Shutterstock, 10-11; Ben Welsh/Axiom Photographic/Design Pics/SuperStock, 12; ohsisterstudio/Shutterstock, 13; Gelpi/Shutterstock, 14-15tl; Milan Vachal/Shutterstock, 14-15tr; Ondrej Prosicky/Shutterstock, 14-15bl; michael sheehan/Shutterstock, 14-15br; Pivliha/iStock, 16-17; JOAT/Shutterstock, 18; tbralnina/iStock, 19; Wolfgang Kaehler/SuperStock, 20-21; Philip Lange/Shutterstock, 23.

Printed in the United States of America at Corporate Graphics in North Mankato, Minnesota.

TABLE OF CONTENTS

CHAPTER 1
Welcome to Morocco!...................................4

CHAPTER 2
Land and Animals....................................12

CHAPTER 3
Life in Morocco.......................................18

QUICK FACTS & TOOLS
At a Glance..22
Glossary..23
Index..24
To Learn More..24

CHAPTER 1

WELCOME TO MOROCCO!

ksar

See a ksar. This group of clay buildings is more than 300 years old! It is in Ait-Ben-Haddou in Morocco. High walls surround it.

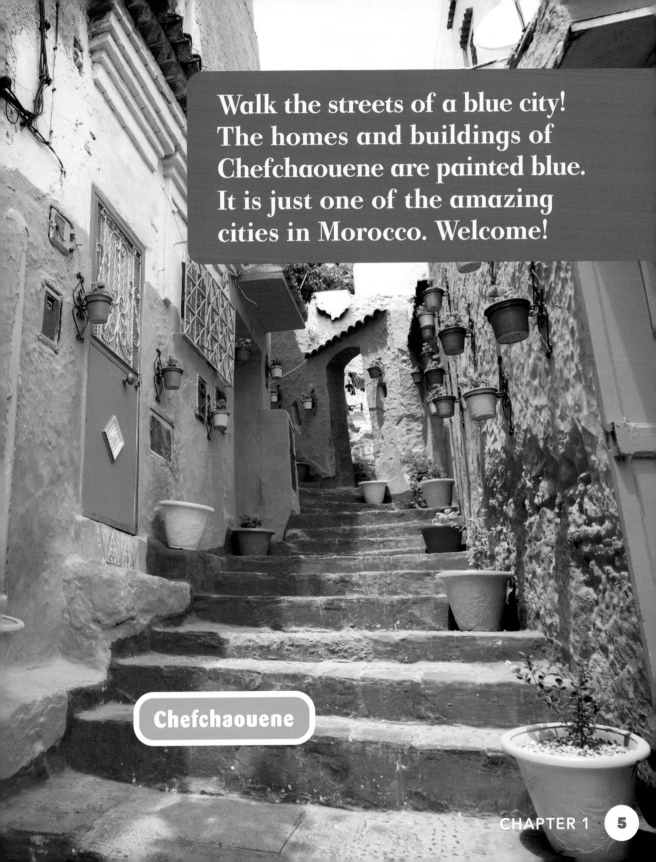

Walk the streets of a blue city! The homes and buildings of Chefchaouene are painted blue. It is just one of the amazing cities in Morocco. Welcome!

Chefchaouene

Mausoleum of King Mohammed V

Rabat is the **capital**.
The **Mausoleum** of
King Mohammed V is here.
He and his two sons are
buried in it. A decorated
dome is inside.

DID YOU KNOW?

The king of Morocco is chief of state. He approves all decisions. He chooses a **prime minister** to lead the country.

Casablanca is the most **populated** city in Morocco. It is a **port** city. Many **exports** are shipped from here. Like what? Clothing, fruits, fish, and cars are some.

Casablanca

souk

Almost every town has a souk. This is an open-air market. Food, clothes, toys, rugs, and more are sold. You might see jugglers or a snake charmer!

TAKE A LOOK!

Souks are often organized by what they sell. What are some of the things you can shop for? Take a look!

textiles

jewelry

spices

pottery

rugs

fabric

CHAPTER 2

LAND AND ANIMALS

Would you like to go surfing? Morocco is on Africa's northern coast. It borders both the Atlantic Ocean and the Mediterranean Sea. People gather at beaches for swimming and picnics. See people kitesurfing!

Mount Toubkal

The highest point here is Mount Toubkal. It is 13,665 feet (4,165 meters) high. This peak is in the southern Atlas Mountains. The Rif Mountains are in the north.

stork

pelican

flamingo

cattle egret

Migrating birds rest in Morocco. Why? The **climate** is warm. You will see storks and pelicans. You might spot flamingos and cattle egrets, too!

The Anti-Atlas Mountains are near Western Sahara Desert. This is a **territory** of Morocco.

Would you like to camp in a desert tent? You can do that here!

WHAT DO YOU THINK?

People travel on camels in the desert. Why? Camels have wide feet. It is easier for them to walk in the sand. How do you get from place to place?

desert tent

CHAPTER 3

LIFE IN MOROCCO

Most people here celebrate Ramadan. Eid al-Fitr marks the end of it. Another holy festival is Eid al-Adha. People visit one another. They exchange gifts.

tajine

couscous

Tajine is a meat stew. Paprika and cinnamon flavor it. Hot peppers and garlic are also in it. Couscous is served with it. Mint tea is the **national** drink. Yum!

Most children begin school when they are seven years old. Many girls wear white smocks. Boys wear blue. Children must attend school until they are 13. Some continue schooling after that. Others help at home.

There is always something new to see in Morocco. Would you like to visit?

WHAT DO YOU THINK?

Students go home every day to eat lunch with their families. Then they return to school. Who do you eat lunch with during the school day? Would you like to eat with your family?

smock

QUICK FACTS & TOOLS

MOROCCO

Location: northern Africa

Size: 172,414 square miles (446,550 square kilometers)

Population: 34,314,130 (July 2018 estimate)

Capital: Rabat

Type of Government: parliamentary constitutional monarchy

Languages: Arabic, French, Berber languages

Exports: clothing and textiles, automobiles, petroleum products, citrus fruits, vegetables, fish

Currency: Moroccan dirham

GLOSSARY

capital: A city where government leaders meet.

climate: The weather typical of a certain place over a long period of time.

exports: Products sold to different countries.

mausoleum: A large room or building for holding a dead body.

migrating: Moving to another area or climate at a particular time of year.

national: Of, having to do with, or shared by a whole nation.

populated: Having people living in it.

port: A town with a harbor where ships can load and unload goods.

prime minister: The leader of a country.

territory: Land under the control of a state, nation, or ruler.

Morocco's currency

INDEX

Ait-Ben-Haddou 4

Anti-Atlas Mountains 16

Atlantic Ocean 12

Atlas Mountains 13

birds 15

camels 16

Casablanca 8

Chefchaouene 5

children 20

climate 15

Eid al-Adha 18

Eid al-Fitr 18

exports 8

food 10, 19

king 7

ksar 4

Mausoleum of King Mohammed V 7

Mediterranean Sea 12

Mount Toubkal 13

prime minister 7

Rabat 7

Ramadan 18

Rif Mountains 13

school 20

souk 10, 11

Western Sahara Desert 16

TO LEARN MORE

Finding more information is as easy as 1, 2, 3.

1 Go to www.factsurfer.com

2 Enter "Morocco" into the search box.

3 Click the "Surf" button to see a list of websites.

FACT SURFER